MW00675944

The Unlimited Realm
Volume 2

Warren Hunter

Sword Ministries International
Branson, Missouri

Unless otherwise indicated, all scriptural quotations are from *The New King James Version* of the Bible, Copyright © 1982 by Thomas Nelson, Inc.

Scripture verses marked KNOX are taken from *The New Testament in the Translation of Monsignor Ronald Knox.*

Scripture verses marked RSV are taken from the *Revised Standard Version,* Old Testament Section, Copyright © 1952, New Testament Section, Copyright © 1946 by Division of Christian Education of the National Council of the Churches of Christ in the U.S.A.

Scripture verses marked NIV are taken from the *New International Version* of the Bible, Copyright © 1973, 1978 by International Bible Society.

The Unlimited Realm Volume 2
Published by:
Sword Ministries International
3044 Shepherd of the Hills
Exprwy Ste 649
Branson, MO 65616
ISBN 1-889816-02-7

Copyright © 1999 by Warren Hunter
All rights reserved.
Reproduction of text in whole or in part without the express written consent by the author is not permitted and is unlawful according to the 1976 United States Copyright Act.

Cover design & book production by:
DB & Associates Design & Distribution
dba Double Blessing Productions
P.O. Box 52756, Tulsa, OK 74152
www.dbassoc.org
Cover illustration is protected by the 1976 United States Copyright Act.
Copyright © 1999 by DB & Associates Design Group, Inc.

Printed in the United States of America.

Contents

Introduction

I truly believe that God desires to launch the body of Christ into the fullness that God has ordained for us since time began. However, there is no way we are going to break into all that God has for us unless we know both where and how to start. One of the problems is that many are afraid to start, because when they have started in the past, they experienced opposition.

Why should that come as a surprise? That is the nature of moving *forward*.

When a vehicle moves forward, it experiences a force caused by wind resistance known as drag. However, you will not feel anything when standing still. But, if you are walking you are going to feel some resistance. If you are running, you are going to feel a little more resistance. When you get on a motorbike and start moving down the road at high speeds, you can really feel the wind coming against you. Thus, resistance is natural when one is making progress.

Indeed, God has a plan for each of us, but it will not come to pass until we get up and do something about it.

Anytime a rocket is launched and breaks through the radiation barrier, it has to break free from the gravitational pull of the earth, and this brings up an interesting analogy. The earth's gravity reminds me of the pull of the world's system, and the rocket engines remind me of the force of God's love. The world is always going to try to grip us and hold us down. But if we want to launch into the love of God and into the unlimited realm of what God has for us, then we must break free from the love of the world.

The love of God quite simply must be *stronger* in us than the love of this world.

To understand the purpose and the love of God, and to come into His unlimited love, we have to deal with our own motives and outlook. We have to ask ourselves what is most important to us? What is most essential in our life? Jesus dealt with this issue in one sense when he was asked which is the great commandment.

Then one of them, a lawyer, asked Him a question, testing Him, and saying,

"Teacher, which is the great commandment in the law?"

Jesus said to him, "'You shall love the Lord your God with all your heart, with all your soul, and with all your mind.'

"This is the first and great commandment.

"And the second is like it: 'You shall love your neighbor as yourself.'

"On these two commandments hang all the Law and the Prophets."

Matthew 22:35-40

It's amazing to think that virtually every principle in God's Word depends on loving God with all of our hearts and loving others as we do ourselves. Right from the lips of Christ one can see that the power is in His love, and it's love that's going to move us into the unlimited realms of God. In love, the gifts of the Spirit will flow.

In love, compassion can have its free reign.

In love, we'll be able to do what God has called us to do.

Love will lead us and bring us into the place where God can release His creative power through us.

But our motive and our desire must be love, because only love will break the barriers we're faced with. And make no mistake, if we want to get what God has for us we have to break through several barriers of resistance.

What are we going to encounter as resistance? Offenses, bitterness, and anxiety to name a few. In fact, there are many things that are going to come along to try to stop us from what God has for us. Before we can step into unlimited love we have to deal with other issues, especially the issue of *forgiveness.*

In the first volume, we dealt with unlimited knowledge and unlimited vision. Those two things are very important as a foundation for this text. We need to get the knowledge of forgiveness and the knowledge of love, as well as the vision of forgiveness and the vision of love, in order to see clearly where God is leading us. He's getting ready to launch us into the place where His love can propel us with absolute freedom. This is a place where there will be no hindrances, no barriers, nothing holding us back.

Chapter 1
Unlimited Forgiveness

Our Choice

God's love is never going to flow properly unless there is unlimited forgiveness: a godly forgiveness that flows from the heart freely, like a river.

We have to break free from the offenses, the bitterness, and the anxiety. We have to leave all things behind and press on toward the new things of God.

I believe that God is actively trying to assist us in breaking free, but we must be willing to *choose* to break free ourselves. Think for a moment about how much thought and planning went into the design of the space shuttle to enable it to break through the radiation barrier. The shuttle had all of the necessary equipment, but if the pilots and operators did not set into motion the launch plans, the shuttle would never have even been launched.

Similarly, God has designed us equipped and internally secure to be able to break through to the realms of His omnipotence, omnipresence, and omniscience. Nevertheless, we must choose to launch out by allowing His forgiveness and love to flow.

Furthermore, we must learn to reject all bitterness brought on by the offenses of other people and circumstances. It's important to also deal with bitterness in this chapter because bitterness and unforgiveness are very

1

similar satanic tools used against the church. They're similar in the way they function, as each tries to gain a foothold and grow, but *God's unlimited forgiveness* is the answer.

He has already set the plans of forgiveness in place. He has already set His love in place so that we can break through the offenses, the bitterness, and the anxiety. He has given us many biblical examples of breaking through Satan's traps. Nevertheless, it's also important to remember that He will never *force* us to walk in love and forgiveness.

Moses

In the Old Testament, starting with Genesis, there are only a few good examples of people walking in unlimited forgiveness. One of the greatest of these is Moses. Although he had a lot of offenses, obstacles, bitterness, anxiety, and worry to overcome, he still managed to break through to the place where God was leading him.

Indeed, depending on how one looks at it, there were many things over which Moses could have become bitter. His real mother abandoned him, leaving him floating on the river when he was an infant. He was raised by foster parents who were not of his own people or his own culture. He was raised in the occult practices and knowledge of false gods that were popular in Egypt at the time. Without considering God's plan, all of these things could be misconstrued, causing him to become very bitter.

As a young man, he later realizes the calling of God in his life, and he begins to resent the oppression of his people. Now he has to deal with this, too. He grew up as a privileged Egyptian, separated from those he now cares about. How can he fulfill the calling in his heart to help them? He soon finds a way. He sees an Egyptian beating a Hebrew slave and he kills the Egyptian in the heat of emotions. Now he really has a reason to be bitter.

He has attempted to fulfill God's plan on his life in the arm of the flesh. He ran ahead of the plans of God. Now he is wanted as a murderer!

Afterwards, Moses runs out into the wilderness thinking to himself, "Oh Lord, I killed a man." The guilt of murdering a man must have been unbearable. Sitting out there in the backside of the wilderness he must have been thinking, "I really messed up." There were now many, many barriers to break through. He could have thought to himself, "I was abandoned as a child, raised by foster parents in satanic practices, and now I am wanted for murder; I have a right to be bitter."

We would never have heard about Moses if he had allowed bitterness and unforgiveness to destroy and possess him on the inside. On the other hand, he could choose not to be bitter and allow God to fulfill that calling he felt in his heart. After all, it was out of faith and love that his mother hid him, hoping the Egyptians would find him and spare his life. Perhaps the schooling in Egypt was preparation for leadership and perhaps his action in killing the Egyptian was a fleshly reaction to something greater that God had placed within his heart.

After many years, and many obstacles to overcome, things started to change. Moses hears from God in the wilderness. He then warns Pharaoh of God's wrath, if he doesn't let the Hebrews go. Finally, he leads the people out of Egypt and faces the Red Sea with the Egyptian army coming from behind. Without hesitation, He tells the children of Israel to stand still and see the salvation of the Lord.

At the same time, the Hebrews are facing many barriers of their own. One such problem was abusive leadership, which bred fear and distrust of those in authority. "You brought us this far to kill us," they tell him, "why don't you just let us go back to Egypt and be slaves like we were before." (Here we can see the

3

previously mentioned rocket going nowhere right now, just sitting at the launch site, powerless.)

Moses has the Red Sea in front of him and the Egyptian army behind him. As if those challenges are not enough, the very people he has had on his heart for years are grumbling and complaining.

Now, he *has* to put into practice *God's unlimited forgiveness.*

He has to stay in an attitude of forgiveness and love. But did this attitude begin at the Red Sea? No! If Moses would have waited to practice forgiveness until then, he would not have been prepared for dealing with this very stubborn and bitter group of people.

In the midst of all that he went through in his early life, the power of forgiveness and love were being developed on the inside.

Afterwards, they go through the wilderness, and even after God's mighty acts of deliverance, the children of Israel still don't stop their childish complaining. Their attitude makes a trip that should have taken at most a couple of weeks turn into forty years of wandering in the wilderness.

The School of Forgiveness

Forgiveness is in one sense a *yardstick to spiritual maturity.*

In other words, forgiveness is going to determine *how mature we are in God.*

Moses had by this time matured a great deal, but he had to be trained. Like Moses, we too have to go through the *school* of forgiveness and that means we have to have something to forgive. That means somebody has to do us wrong, stab us in the back, or abuse us in some way. Of course, that shouldn't be much of a problem. Most of us have had *numerous* opportunities to begin practicing unlimited forgiveness.

I remember all the things I personally went through in life. My first mom died when I was only six and my step mom died when I was fourteen. Through all of this there was tremendous strife, confusion, and anger in our home, which led to excessive over-discipline and much abuse in this area. This left our family to work through tremendous forgiveness. We had to learn to obtain a clearer picture of love through the help of the Holy Spirit.

A little later in life I moved to a brand new country and experienced both language and cultural shock. At college, I was constantly inundated with a variety of misunderstandings and criticisms. And then, when I finally went into full-time ministry, do you suppose the problems all ceased? If you do, think again.

In ministry, I've had people throw things at me while preaching, curse at me, and perhaps worst of all, I've had many ministers stab me in the back.

It's one thing when the world does you wrong, but it's quite another thing when the people of God that are all around you, the so-called children of God, mistreat you.

Naturally, it wasn't God's perfect will for all of these things to happen. God wasn't going around killing my relatives and making people abuse me to teach me something. But he does *use* these things and turn them around for His glory.

All along, this *school of forgiveness* was doing something on the inside. Rather than developing the power of bitterness, it was developing the power of forgiveness. God was bringing me to a place of greater maturity where his unlimited forgiveness could flow.

Forgive Their Sin

Moses comes to this place in Exodus 32. He went through the Red Sea and all kinds of other things, and the children of Israel were still grumbling and complaining. He went through the water from the rock, Mt. Sinai, the golden calf, and passed through the fire. If there was ever a time when Moses could've been unforgiving, this would've been the perfect time. The Israelites just didn't want to obey God. They were rebellious all of the time.

Finally, in Exodus 32, we see the ultimate test that I believe reveals *unlimited forgiveness*. Remember that Moses had passed through all kinds of barriers. By the time we get to Exodus 32, the children of Israel have really messed up. It was here that they built the golden calf.

And the LORD said to Moses, "Go, get down! For your people whom you brought out of the land of Egypt have corrupted themselves.

"They have turned aside quickly out of the way which I commanded them. They have made themselves a molded calf, and worshiped it and sacrificed to it, and said, 'This is your god, O Israel, that brought you out of the land of Egypt!'"

And the LORD said to Moses, "I have seen this people, and indeed it is a stiff-necked people!

"Now therefore, let Me alone, that My wrath may burn hot against them and I may consume them. And I will make of you a great nation."

Then Moses pleaded with the LORD his God, and said: "LORD, why does Your wrath burn hot against Your people whom You have brought out of the land of Egypt with great power and with a mighty hand?

"Why should the Egyptians speak, and say, 'He brought them out to harm them, to kill them in the mountains, and to consume them from the face of the earth'? Turn from Your fierce wrath, and relent from this harm to Your people.

"Remember Abraham, Isaac, and Israel, Your servants, to whom You swore by Your own self, and said to them, 'I will multiply your descendants as the stars of heaven; and all this land that I have spoken of I give to your descendants, and they shall inherit it forever.'"

So the LORD relented from the harm which He said He would do to His people.

Then Moses returned to the LORD and said, "Oh, these people have committed a great sin, and have made for themselves a god of gold!

"Yet now, if You will forgive their sin — but if not, I pray, blot me out of Your book which You have written."

Exodus 32:7-14,31,32

He could've said, "Look at them God, I'm up here in the glory with You for forty days, and as soon as I turn my back they're down there building a golden calf." But that wasn't his attitude. He just kept going on in forgiveness.

Let's paraphrase that last verse: "God, if You don't forgive these people, take my name out of the Lamb's Book of Life. I'm prepared to go to hell for them." That's the power of unlimited forgiveness.

Moses had come to that place that is so powerful, the place of absolute forgiveness. How many of us are prepared to go to hell to forgive the very person that offended us?

It takes a lot of maturity to come to a place where the power of forgiveness comes to full fruition. There are many barriers to break. I've found it very important to remember that God forgives us more than just about anything else that He does for us. I've also found out that we'll never experience *all* that God has for us until we learn to walk in this kind of forgiveness. It's powerful.

Miriam and Aaron

Again we see Moses in Numbers 12. Now it's his own family, Aaron and Miriam, who've come against him.

Then Miriam and Aaron spoke against Moses because of the Ethiopian woman whom he had married; for he had married an Ethiopian woman.

So they said, "Has the LORD indeed spoken only through Moses? Has he not spoken through us also?" And the LORD heard it.

(Now the man Moses was very humble, more than all men who were on the face of the earth.)

Suddenly the LORD said to Moses, Aaron, and Miriam, "Come out, you three, to the tabernacle of meeting!" So the three came out.

Then the LORD came down in the pillar of cloud and stood in the door of the tabernacle, and called Aaron and Miriam. And they both went forward.

then He said, "Hear now My words: If there is a prophet among you, I, the LORD, make Myself known to him in a vision; I speak to him in a dream.

Not so with my servant Moses; he is faithful in all My house.

I speak with him face to face, even plainly, and not in dark sayings; and he sees the form of the

LORD. Why then were you not afraid to speak against My servant Moses?"

So the anger of the LORD was aroused against them, and He departed.

And when the cloud departed from above the tabernacle, suddenly Miriam became leprous, as white as snow....
                                            Numbers 12:1-10

But Moses is still full of forgiveness, even though they were passing judgement on him.

And Moses cried unto the LORD, saying Heal her now, O God, I beseech thee.
                              Numbers 12:13 (KJV)

Afterwards, God honors Moses' request and heals her. Why? I believe God healed her because of the power of forgiveness. Moses never stopped walking in the power of forgiveness.

We'll never accomplish anything for God if we don't learn to walk in forgiveness. Kathryn Kuhlman used to say, "Do you really want to know the Holy Spirit? He costs everything." In like manner, we need to understand the high price of forgiveness. Not only did it cost Jesus everything, it will cost *us* everything as well.

I've seen many people come to revivals and get upset at something that was said or done. Then they will often get up and leave early, both mad and offended. Why do people get offended so easily? Their behavior provides insight into how deep their forgiveness goes.

The Forgiveness of God

Remember that Jesus Christ is our perfect and complete example in all matters of faith and conduct, and the Old Testament is a type and shadow of the New Testament. Nevertheless, despite the fact that Jesus was God incarnate, everywhere Jesus walked, people were offended. They did not allow forgiveness to be released, because they were the ones yelling, "Crucify Him." Finally, Jesus died because the people who were offended stirred everybody else up. But in all that, Jesus never gave up on them or on us.

He died because He loved us. He forgave us for all our sins and cleansed us from all unrighteousness. Thank God that He has forgiven us for all our sins. He has forgiven us a great and mighty debt, a debt that we ourselves could not hope to ever pay. He forgave us.

Recall the parable of the man who owed a tremendous debt and in turn, another owed him a very small debt. When the first man's debt was cancelled, he didn't cancel the smaller debt that was owed to him. After receiving mercy, he went to a fellow servant and demanded full payment, even putting him in prison until he could pay. Needless to say, the king was very angry when he found out what had happened.

"Then his master, after he had called him, said to him, 'You wicked servant! I forgave you all that debt because you begged me.

'Should you not also have had compassion on your fellow servant, just as I had pity on you?'

"And his master was angry, and delivered him to the torturers until he should pay all that was due to him.

"So My heavenly Father also will do to you if each of you, from his heart, does not forgive his brother his trespasses."

Matthew 18:32-35

Notice that Jesus states where forgiveness comes from; it *must* come from the heart. There is power in forgiveness, but there's only pain and heartache in unforgiveness.

The truth of the matter is, both bitterness and unforgiveness will hurt the one who holds onto them far more than the one against whom it's held.

In Matthew chapter six, Jesus proclaims, "If you don't forgive men, neither will My Father forgive you your transgressions." Jesus even prayed when He was dying on the cross, "Father forgive them for they know not what they do."

That ultimate act of forgiveness launched something *so* powerful; it literally set God's forgiveness in place for all eternity.

God is waiting to show His mercy and His forgiveness and His love to us. When He died, He forgave our sins, and today he still forgives our sins.

That power of forgiveness has been released, and it can *never* return void.

God is waiting for us to accept His forgiveness and the price that He paid for us. In God's throne, unforgiveness is totally destroyed because we're standing in the presence of the great Forgiver. There's nothing that can hold us back when we take to heart the forgiveness of God.

God wants us to move forward with Him to that higher place. He wants us to move past the hurts of the past. He wants to bring us to a place where our hearts can be consecrated and set apart for Him, where we can learn to walk in forgiveness towards all who have offended us.

A Foundation of Forgiveness

Unforgiveness cripples our heart's ability to express love freely, especially against those who've hurt us. If gone unchecked, unforgiveness will essentially begin to rule the heart. It will keep the heart from expressing forgiveness and releasing what God has for us.

In fact, I believe God is able to bless us only to the extent that we're able to bless those whom we *least* likely want to bless.

We have to enter a perpetual *state of forgiveness.* We have to set a *foundation of forgiveness.*

He remembers our sins no more. I believe that when the love of God is shed abroad in our hearts (Romans 5:5), the nature of the forgiver must become our nature because God Himself has placed it within us.

When released, the power of forgiveness will flow, unlike unforgiveness which stops the anointing. When there's a release of unlimited *forgiveness,* there's also a release of God's unlimited *love,* and subsequently a release in the free flow of the unlimited *anointing.*

I believe that God's forgiveness serves as a foundation for all of these other things. If we retain anger and bitterness, we hinder ourselves in these other areas.

"Therefore if you bring your gift to the altar, and there remember that your brother has something against you,

"leave your gift there before the altar, and go your way. First be reconciled to your brother, and then come and offer your gift."

Matthew 5:23,24

When we're not against anybody, and we're not offended, we're prepared to release the love of God freely. Jesus tells us in Matthew 18:20, "How many times must we forgive? Seventy times seven."

Forgiveness Sets Miracles in Motion

Aside from Jesus, Stephen is one of the finest examples of unlimited forgiveness. In the book of Acts, he's questioned by an angry mob and is about to be stoned to death. But notice the attitude of his heart:

When they heard these things they were cut to the heart, and they gnashed at him with their teeth.

But he, being full of the Holy Spirit, gazed into heaven and saw the glory of God, and Jesus standing at the right hand of God,

and said, "Look! I see the heavens opened and the Son of Man standing at the right hand of God!"

Then they cried out with a loud voice, stopped their ears, and ran at him with one accord;

and they cast him out of the city and stoned him. And the witnesses laid down their clothes at the feet of a young man named Saul.

And they stoned Stephen as he was calling on God and saying, "Lord Jesus, receive my spirit."

Then he knelt down and cried out with a loud voice, "Lord, do not charge them with this sin." And when he had said this, he fell asleep.

Acts 7:54-60

The power of forgiveness was released. Forgiveness and love even affected his perception. He saw Jesus standing ready to receive him.

But there was a man standing there called Saul. He was holding the robes of those stoning Stephen. Stephen asked the Lord to forgive them, and that included Saul. He asked God to forgive them while Saul was standing there watching the whole process. He was holding the cloaks, he was participating in it. But Stephen said, "Lord, do not charge them with this sin." The power of forgiveness was released just like the day Jesus died and shed His blood on the cross.

13

Although Saul got up and began to wreak havoc on the Church, God was sitting in heaven saying, "Saul, Stephen has released the power of forgiveness to you...he forgave you for stoning him...he forgave you for persecuting Christ."

That power of forgiveness was so strong in Stephen's life that it set into motion Paul's Road to Damascus experience. I sincerely believe that Paul would never have been converted and later wrote the many great books of the Bible that he did *had Stephen* not forgiven him that day.

If we forgive the people that hurt us, we also are going to set into motion the Road to Damascus experience for them. God wants to save them, too. God wants to heal them and deliver them. However, God often wants to use the very person who has been wronged to minister forgiveness. God wants to use us powerfully, as well as them.

Stephen released the power of forgiveness and set the experience of Paul on the road to Damascus into motion. As a result, I believe that Stephen had a share in all of the work that Paul accomplished for God's kingdom after his stoning.

We can have that same foundation of unlimited forgiveness in our own lives. The equipment is all in place. But we must choose to launch this spiritual rocket by releasing the forgiveness that will propel us and others further than we have ever gone before.

Chapter 2
Unlimited Love

God is Love

Beloved, let us love one another, for love is of God; and everyone who loves is born of God and knows God.

He who does not love does not know God, for God is love.

In this the love of God was manifested toward us, that God has sent His only begotten Son into the world, that we might live through Him.

1 John 4:7-9

God not only loves us, He *is* love. In order to grow in our relationship with God, we need to understand that God is love. Notice that the Bible never says that God is faith or hope. The Bible says that Christ may dwell in your heart *through* faith that you may be rooted and grounded in love.

The way the anointing is going to dwell in our hearts is through faith that is rooted and grounded in love. And I cannot emphasize enough that the means by which we are going to receive this is *in love*.

Paul writes in First Corinthians chapter 13, now abide faith, hope, and love, but the greatest of these is *love*. Love is the greatest, because God is love. He is the

God *of* faith and hope, but He *is* love. Notice the key words here are *of* and *is*.

Any Christian would agree that God is unlimited because he is omnipresent and omniscient, as well as omnipotent. Yet if all this is true, love must also be unlimited because God is love.

Since God's love is unlimited in power, love is the force that is going to propel us into the unlimited realms of God.

Key to the Miraculous

Love is a key to the miraculous that many people overlook. Miracles are going to happen through faith, *out of love.* Love has got to be our motive. Why? Because there's nothing that can stop us from doing what God has called us to do when we operate in love. There is no boundary that can stand in the path of love. No one can bind love. No one can stop love. Miracles happen when God's children are moving in faith propelled *by love.*

Wherever we love the most, that's where we are going to have the most amount of miracles. Being a native of South Africa, I have had many opportunities to minister there, and also to speak to others who have ministered there. Quite frequently, I've had different ministers tell me that they have more miracles in Africa than in the United States. I personally believe this is because they go with hearts full of the love of God, expecting God to do miracles. They see less miracles at home because their love does not have the same intensity.

Many ministers get tired of their home churches in America, having to lay hands on the same people every Sunday. By the time they get to Africa, they see new people hungry for God, with new problems and new needs. Suddenly, the compassion of God rises on the inside of them and they feel more sensitive to those people, so guess what happens? They get more miracles.

If this is difficult to believe, look at it this way. Remember that 1 Corinthians 13 reveals to us that love is both patient and kind. Have you ever noticed how many Christians are less patient and less kind to the ones to whom they are the closest, their own families? And why is it sometimes easier to be patient and kind with complete strangers from another continent?

Far too often, Christians allow *familiarity* to cool the love of God in their hearts.

Agape

In love is God's power. Hate cannot remain in love's presence; sickness and infirmity cannot stay. Love will drive out anything that's unlike Christ. There's something that's so powerful about love that it simply can't be stopped.

I've noticed that a lot of people don't understand the ramifications of God's love, or the dimensions of it. As the previous verse in First John states, God is love. The Greek word that is translated love in this particular verse is *agape*. *Agape* is not something that is a feeling and it's not simply a physical experience. The Greek words that express these ideas are *phileo*, which is an affectionate type of love, and *eros*, which is a more passionate kind of love.[1] On the other hand, *agape* is a word that describes God's love for us. This kind of love is very unselfish and can bring discernment into every situation.

Love Is...

In 1 Corinthians 13, the apostle Paul renders a beautifully inspired definition of *agape*. This chapter is perhaps one of the most important chapters in the Bible.

Though I speak with the tongues of men and of angels, but have not love, I have become sounding brass or a clanging cymbal.

And though I have the gift of prophecy, and understand all mysteries and all knowledge, and though I have all faith, so that I could remove mountains, but have not love, I am nothing.

And though I bestow all my goods to feed the poor, and though I give my body to be burned, but have not love, it profits me nothing.

Love suffers long and is kind; love does not envy; love does not parade itself, is not puffed up;

does not behave rudely, does not seek its own, is not provoked, thinks no evil;

does not rejoice in iniquity, but rejoices in the truth;

bears all things, believes all things, hopes all things, endures all things.

Love never fails. But whether there are prophecies, they will fail; whether there are tongues, they will cease; whether there is knowledge, it will vanish away.

And now abide faith, hope, love, these three; but the greatest of these is love.

1 Corinthians 13:1-8,13

The Importance of Love

Love sheds light on the unknown. There's nothing hidden which will not be revealed. Love turns the light bulb of God's glory on. Get the revelation that there's nothing that's going to stop the power of God's love.

God's book is a book of love. God's plan is a plan of love. His destiny for us is a destiny of love. His purpose is a purpose of love.

Everything that He has done, and everything that He has accomplished or will do, He began in love. It was in love that He laid the foundation for our destiny to be by His side. He laid all the foundations of the world in love. He created all things in love.

If we abide in love, we'll abide in God's perfect will. Since there's not one thing that God has done, or will do that's outside of love...we, as His children and His imitators, should do and accomplish everything in love as well. As His children, we should be imitators of Him (Ephesians 5:1). *Why?*...because we're made in His image and likeness (Genesis 1:26).

We should have His attitude of love. I'm not just talking about an occasional thing; I am talking about a motive of love, literally in operation *all of the time*. He wants us to demonstrate His love because His love is so important to who He is and who we are. God wants His love to flow through us in *everything* that we do.

Operating in Love

In some parts of Africa there are villages where approximately eighty percent of the population has AIDS. I remember in Zimbabwe, as we were going out to preach to a tribal group in the bush, a little boy suddenly came running out of the bush and said in his native language, "My mom has been lying out in the sun all day long and she is dying." After the translator interpreted the boy's words, I ran over to the bush, and true to his word, there was a lady about eight months pregnant lying on the ground dying of AIDS.

Immediately the guy with me, who managed a medical clinic, confirmed my observation. Lying next to

19

her was a little baby about a year old, another one two years old, and a third one about three years old, all lying in the sun sleeping. In addition to these, she had three other children ages five, nine, and eleven. Apparently, they had been lying there for about a day and a half. The children had been going out in the field collecting grasshoppers to eat, the whereabouts of their dad was unknown.

The pastor I was with shared with me how most of the women in this part of Africa are virtually slaves that do everything. That's why it was most devastating to a family when the mother died.

As soon as we came upon the scene, I sensed in my spirit that this lady would be dead before the end of the day. So, I stretched my body over her and began to pray. As I prayed for her, I soon began to weep and cry. In faith, energized by love, I began releasing the anointing.

What happened next is difficult to describe with words. In much the same way that faith can rise up and fill the heart, *the love of God* rose up inside of me. Love began to operate in a new dimension. I was led by the Spirit to command a blood transfusion. I did this for about fifteen minutes or so until the power of God hit her.

Then, she rose up quickly, strengthened in her body and *absolutely healed*.

Several days later they took her to the clinic and verified that she no longer had AIDS. Through the power of His love, working through faith, God moved through me to totally heal that lady of AIDS.

God is looking for people who will operate in love. He's waiting for people to rise up and say, "God we're tired of sickness; we're tired of disease and pain. We're going to see the power of God flow in that person; and we're going to do *whatever* it takes to have a miracle."

Reaching Out

John Wesley once made the statement that love drives one forward into the unknown, tumultuous human experience around us.

I believe that is an excellent description. Love *is* outgoing. Love *is* outreached. Love *pours* itself out.

Love has *nothing* selfish within it. It always wants to bless; it always wants to help; and it always wants to stretch forth to touch those around it. Love goes beyond anything else in the world. There's a place love can go where nothing else can.

In the Spirit

who also declared to us your love in the Spirit.
Colossians 1:8

Notice it says "your love *in the Spirit*." There is a love in the Spirit. It's not just a love from self, it's a love in the Spirit. Recall that the Bible says, those who worship God must worship Him in Spirit and in truth. Since this is the case, then it seems only logical that God's love must come from the Spirit. Indeed the Spirit has a very special role, as is evident in verses such as the following from Romans:

Now hope does not disappoint, because the love of God has been poured out in our hearts by the Holy Spirit who was given to us.
Romans 5:5

The Holy Spirit is the one pouring out God's love within our hearts. I love when Song of Solomon speaks of his beloved and says that she has dove eyes. A dove represents the Holy Spirit. It's like Jesus saying to His

Bride the Church, "I see that your eyes are full of the Spirit of God, and that the love of God is abounding inside of you." Imagine the Lord saying that to us. "I see dove eyes in you, my bride." I believe that the Lord is longing to say that to His Church today.

Increasing in Love

And may the Lord make you increase and abound in love to one another and to all, just as we do to you.
1 Thessalonians 3:12

As we can see from this verse, love is something that we must increase and abound in. Not only does God desire for us to increase and abound in love, he can assist us, because all love *must* come through the Spirit, *from* God Himself.

But concerning brotherly love you have no need that I should write to you, for you yourselves are taught by God to love one another.
1 Thessalonians 4:9

God is the one who is going to teach us about His love. It's not because we're trying to exercise it in our own effort or our own ability. It's something that comes from *spending time with God* because God is love. If we want the love of God to rub off on us, we have to hang around with the ultimate lover.

God is love and God is a lover. The more time we spend in His presence, the more loving we become. The more time we spend in His presence, the more we begin to understand the limitless dimensions of His love.

The Bible reveals to us plainly that it's God who teaches us to love. He wants to teach us to move in an unlimited realm of love. We're not supposed to be ignorant of love, because God will teach us.

Now may the Lord direct your hearts into the love of God and into the patience of Christ.

2 Thessalonians 3:5

In this scripture, the Apostle Paul picks up on something very important. He writes, "may the Lord direct your hearts into the love of God." Paul is praying that God will bring the *focus* of your heart into His love.

That is the secret of increasing in the love of God, for us to become focused on it. Indeed, anyone would agree, the more you focus on something, the more it increases. This is obvious with sins of the flesh, but it's especially so with the love of God.

In this, Paul understood that when our hearts were set on God's love, it would thrive and increase, and nothing else could stop us. God has a destiny and a direction for us, and that's for us to be focused on Him so that we'll flow in His love.

that Christ may dwell in your hearts through faith; that you, being rooted and grounded in love,

may be able to comprehend with all the saints what is the width and length and depth and height —

to know the love of Christ which passes knowledge; that you may be filled with all the fullness of God.

Ephesians 3:17-19

How are we going to be filled with all the fullness of God? By understanding the *dimensions* of the love of Christ. The dimensions, or the width, length, depth, and height, are incredibly vast.

The good news, however, is that God *wants* us to comprehend it. In essence, Paul is praying that we comprehend the incomprehensible. The only way that we can do that is by acknowledging that we are called by God Himself to act upon His unction.

Knowing that it's God's will for us to know this, we can be sure that we're thereby anointed to comprehend and move in His love.

Recall that the anointing destroys burdens and removes yokes. What better way to do this than through the power of love? Knowing this, it becomes all the more apparent that love and the anointing have a unique connection. The anointing is inevitably tied to love because *love is unlimited.*

Advantages of Love

There are so many advantages in love. Love casts out fear and reveals the unknown. God does *not* want us to be afraid of the unknown. We'll see when trouble, sickness, and disease are coming, because we're walking in the realms of God's love.

The Bible says perfect love casts out all fear. Love accomplishes this by shining the light of God on the unknown.

Love will also cause us to operate in the gifts of the Spirit, because the gifts involve compassion, God's love. Signs and wonders flow unhindered when they proceed out of love.

And though I have the gift of prophecy, and understand all mysteries and all knowledge, and though I have all faith, so that I could remove mountains, but have not love, I am nothing.

1 Corinthians 13:2

Love will bring us into all wisdom and discernment. Word of knowledge will flow as we operate in love, because *all* of the gifts were designed to function out of love. Gifts like *word of knowledge* and *word of wisdom* sometimes dig dirt up on people, but were not at all designed to embarrass people or to hurt them. They were designed in love to *help* them.

Love is a motive of the heart, and as such, it sees into the depths of another person's heart. As a result, we are thereby equipped to discern and help people who are in need.

The world would have each of us believe that people who operate in divine love are naive and gullible. Perhaps some would even suggest that those who believe the best of everyone are just plain stupid. However, nothing could be further from the truth.

And this I pray, that your love may abound still more and more in knowledge and all discernment.

Philippians 1:9

Paul's prayer for the Philippians is that their love will abound and increase in knowledge and discernment. To put it plainly, we'll grow wiser than we ever dreamed imaginable when we stay *in love*. Why? The answer is very simple.

When we walk in love, God knows that we won't misuse His knowledge and wisdom; therefore, He will pour it out more freely.

When our motive is love, there are no limits to the other things God can share with us. With love comes trust. Note that Paul is careful to express his desire that they abound *more and more* in knowledge and *all* discernment. He is very careful not to set limits, because love is limitless.

God is saying, "I can see that if I give them more knowledge and wisdom, they're not going to abuse and waste it, nor will they use it on the wrong things. I know that they're going to release it in love, so I'll give them more and more."

When we walk in love, love serves as a guide. Love will help and encourage us along the way. Love will propel us in the direction that God has chosen for us to go. It'll never lead us astray. The Bible never sets a limit on what God's love can do. There's a spirit of discernment operating in those full of the love of God. In fact, the love of God in us can best discern any situation.

Contrary to the opinion of some Christians, one does *not* have to be an ex-alcoholic to help get an alcoholic delivered. All one needs to have is *the anointing* that removes burdens and destroys yokes and the *love* of God to propel that anointing into action.

We don't have to go through everything the world goes through to better understand them, but we do have to have something better, called *love*.

Love's Enemy

Beloved, if God so loved us, we also ought to love one another.

No one has seen God at any time. If we love one another, God abides in us, and His love has been perfected in us.

1 John 4:11,12

But if you have bitter envy and self-seeking in your hearts, do not boast and lie against the truth.

This wisdom does not descend from above, but is earthly, sensual, demonic.

For where envy and self-seeking exist, confusion and every evil thing are there.

James 3:14-16

We cannot love others and be envious and jealous of them at the same time. Envy is an enemy of love. Envy is being upset because someone was blessed with something that we weren't. On the other hand, we know that love always believes the best of others. It always hopes that others will change, so it never holds unforgiveness.

bears all things, believes all things, hopes all things, endures all things.

1 Corinthians 13:7

Love holds onto and believes the best of others.

The Perfect Weapon

Love will destroy all of our enemies' attacks against us. In the same way that daytime destroys the night, love is a weapon that destroys hate. In fact, love is a weapon that will defeat anything that can come against us. God wants to bring us to the place where we can walk and flow out of love, where *nothing* can stop us.

God's love is also the perfect weapon against fear, because perfect love casts out fear. The reason people are afraid or anxious is because they have not allowed perfect love to make its dwelling place inside of them. Moreover, the root problem of fear is failure to move in perfect love. Consider that for a moment. If we all did this, we would live our lives to touch others and give ourselves away; we would have absolutely no reason to fear.

With love as our motive, we can't help but be blessed. When we operate and abide in love, it will draw the blessings of God to us.

Time is getting shorter for the body of Christ. We don't have time to remain bound by the limitations brought about by not operating in His love. The perfect bride that Christ is preparing is being perfected in love.

Those who are not allowing Him to perfect them in love are not a part of His body. Love is the *only* way.

A More Excellent Way

But earnestly desire the best gifts. And yet I show you a more excellent way.

Though I speak with the tongues of men and of angels, but have not love, I have become sounding brass or a clanging cymbal.

And though I have the gift of prophecy, and understand all mysteries and all knowledge, and though I have all faith, so that I could remove mountains, but have not love, I am nothing.

And though I bestow all my goods to feed the poor, and though I give my body to be burned, but have not love, it profits me nothing.

1 Corinthians 12:31;13:1,2,3

Many people miss the connection between these two chapters by not realizing that the Bible was not written in chapter and verse. Paul wrote these two chapters to go together, desiring to affirm that the more excellent way *is love*.

Often people will say things like, "I want to go higher with God, or, "I want to understand God more." In response, God is saying, "Fine, I will show you a more excellent way." The more excellent way is walking in love.

The more excellent way is pouring out love, touching others, healing others, ministering to others, setting others free, and doing what God called us to do. *That* is excellency.

Paul proclaimed, "Though I speak with the tongues of men and of angels, but have not love, I have become sounding brass or a clanging cymbal." On the other hand, we can be assured that if we have love, we'll not be a sounding brass or a clanging cymbal. When we have love, we'll have a definite voice full of purpose. We'll have a definite word to build and encourage others. We'll be able to speak into someone's life because we're not speaking from our own selfish motives. When we speak in love, we have the voice of utterance in God's timing and season.

God wants to speak through us. God wants to direct our tongues in His love. He wants us to speak edification, exhortation, and comfort. As previously mentioned, people who walk in love are not gullible or naive. They are bold. It takes chutzpa, or courage, to speak the truth in love. True love will pull people right out of the pits of hell into the realms of God.

In 1994, when my wife and I were ministering in a week revival in Pennsylvania, we experienced that. We were in the middle of the week of services with about three churches together. I felt led to pray for the pastor and his wife and one of their sons. To make a long story short the son was not saved. I had them all hold hands and began to minister to them. When I touched the father's hand, he and his wife hit the floor. Their son still seemed closed. As I walked away I said, "I felt the Holy Spirit directing me to throw a glass of water in their son's face and say 'obey God.'" No sooner had I said this when my wife came up and whispered in my ear that she felt a confirmation that I was to throw the water in the boy's face and tell him to obey God. So that is what I did.

Immediately, the pastor's wife left crying. And what a confrontation my wife and I had with the hosting pastor and his wife after service that night! The pastor's argument was that what I had done was not done in love. My response was, "If you're driving down a road and there's a sign in the road that says, 'Detour, Road Out, Cliff Ahead,' wouldn't you be glad that somebody put it there? Wouldn't you *want* to know that there's a cliff ahead? God was giving your son a final warning sign."

I then sent my wife to speak to the pastor's wife. My wife told her that she knew that we had obeyed God and that we had never done anything like that before. That night the pastor's wife had a dream; and in that dream God reminded her that when their son was younger, he had a paper route, and in order for her to wake him up, he asked her to throw water in his face.

Within a week the boy was saved and his entire life was supernaturally changed. We've not gone back to that church as yet, nor have we gone to *any* of that pastor's churches that were involved in those meetings. But our faith was rooted in love; and our love pulled that boy right out of the pits of hell. Remember, true love confronts.

Faith Working Through Love

For in Christ Jesus neither circumcision nor uncircumcision avails anything, but faith working through love.
Galatians 5:6

Never underestimate the power of faith. It's absolutely necessary to a successful walk with God. In Ephesians chapter 6 Paul likens faith to a shield that can quench all the fiery darts of the enemy.

Without love, we can't even raise that shield, because faith *works through* love. Anyone who desires to operate in faith must be grounded in love.

Note what Smith Wigglesworth states in his book, *The Anointing of His Spirit*, concerning the shield of faith and love: "Love is the trinity working in the human heart to break it, that it may be filled with God's fullness."[1]

Faith works by love. What happens if I *don't* have love? I can't raise the shield of faith to quench all the fiery darts of the wicked one. You might say, "Look now, I have my shield of faith. I'm going to pray for the angels to protect my whole home. I am going to plead the blood of Jesus." But as long as you have no love, you have an open channel through which the enemy can operate. Love will stop the enemy. Love casts out fear. Love will say, "I'm not afraid of what's happening right now." Perfect love will cast out fear. Love raises a barrier that will stop the enemy from coming near what belongs to you.

Love is the energy behind the shield of faith. Many people who feel they're having problems overcoming the enemy, often feel it's because they don't have faith. Although this certainly can be a factor, another possibility exists. Perhaps they need to address whether or not they're truly walking in love. Maybe the problem really isn't what they think it is. Maybe the problem is with their own selfishness, envy, jealousy, unforgiveness, bitterness, hurt, anxiety, and worry. These things can act like a wall that blocks the release of faith, as well as the love of God.

But always remember that *God wants* us to operate in love. *God wants* there to be a release in love that will destroy and break those walls. And if God wants it, *and* we want it, then absolutely nothing can stop the manifestation of it. Satan can never override us when we stand in agreement with almighty God.

Love and Authority

If many Christians were honest, they would admit that they desire more power and authority from God, but the real need is usually love. We already have all of the power and authority we could ever want available to us through love. In love, there is power, authority, and purpose.

God will release His power to the degree that we operate in His love. The more we operate in God's love, the more He will release His power in our direction. When we talk love, when we edify, when we exhort, when we encourage, and when we speak words of life and blessing, God will put more power behind our words and deeds. We'll be acting on God's authority.

If our desire is more of God, and our desire is to be moved in this manner, we must get into God's love *like never before.* Only then will He use us *like never before.*

He will take us where we've never been before, into the unlimited realms of His love. He will give us power like we've never experienced before, but we have to abide in His love. We have to walk in the love of God. We have to make love the focus and centerpiece of our lives. By doing so, we'll make God the focus and centerpiece of our lives, because God is love.

Peace to the brethren, and love with faith, from God the Father and the Lord Jesus Christ.

Ephesians 6:23

To commit to love *forces* spiritual growth.

---

[1]Wayne Warner, *The Anointing of His Spirit* (Servant Publications, 1994), p. 86.

Chapter 3
Unlimited Faith

Smith Wigglesworth said, "With the audacity of faith we should throw ourselves into the omnipotence of God's divine plan; for God has said all things are possible to him who believes."[1]

Quotes by the Author

"Faith works by love. If you have unlimited love, there's no limit to what faith can do. If I have love, I can say to the mountain, "Be moved and be cast into the sea." If I have love, I can raise the shield of faith and quench the fiery darts of the wicked one.

"In the voice of the Father, I sense no doubt or unbelief, but everlasting, unlimited words of faith. These faith words come from His innermost being where overwhelming love continues to swell, fulfilling hopes, stretching beyond all limits of time and space, and bringing the image of hope into place."

Faith is synonymous to trust and confidence. In the New Testament, each of these words are often a translation of the same Greek word. Accordingly, faith almost always involves believing, simply because you can't trust or have confidence in someone if you don't believe in them. In the following verse from Hebrews, you can see how faith and believing God go hand in hand:

> **But without** *faith* **it is impossible to please Him, for he who comes to God must believe that He is, and that He is a rewarder of those who diligently seek Him.**
>
> **Hebrews 11:6**

Faith has become a hotly debated topic among Christians, especially in the last several years. Many have suggested that people in the so called "faith movement" have gone overboard with a subject that's only of limited importance. Obviously, these people have forgotten that without faith it's impossible to please God. I have great difficulty imagining how one could go overboard on something like faith. I sincerely believe that it would be just as hard to go overboard on hope or love. Problems may occur when people focus on faith and exclude the issue of love, but when God's unlimited love is understood and received, one is prepared to launch out into His unlimited faith.

> **For in Christ Jesus neither circumcision nor uncircumcision avails anything, but faith working through love.**
>
> **Galatians 5:6**

> **...Faith that finds its expression in love is all that matters.**
>
> **Galatians 5:6 (KNOX)**

Remember, faith working through love will move mountains (1 Corinthians 13:2). In fact, many people do not realize that faith and love are very similar in some ways, and they often must go hand in hand. For instance, recall in First Corinthians 13:7, Paul writes that love *believes all things*. If love believes all things, then love, in one sense, could require faith.

In other words, you can't really love someone without having a certain amount of faith in them.

As we have already pointed out, faith is also related to believing. For another example, note the connection in the following from Mark:

So Jesus answered and said to them, "Have faith in God.

"For assuredly, I say to you, whoever says to this mountain, 'Be removed and be cast into the sea,' and does not doubt in his heart, but believes that those things he says will be done, he will have whatever he says.

"Therefore I say to you, whatever things you ask when you pray, believe that you receive them, and you will have them."

Mark 11:22-24

Note the phrase from verse 22, "have faith in God." In the Greek manuscript, there is no preposition, leaving one to wonder exactly what the writer meant. Most translations insert the preposition *in* at their own discretion. Some people have no problem with this understanding. On the other hand, some would argue that Jesus was telling His disciples to have the God kind of faith. The God kind of faith shows that there is no limit to it. But at the same time, when we place our faith in God, we are believing in the one who is unlimited.

At any rate, perhaps the main lesson to be learned from this usage is that faith *must* be tied to God. Regardless of whether it is in Him, from Him, or even His kind of faith, faith is not something that leans on its own understanding.

The First and Last Step

Faith has a very special place of importance in our relationship to God. It's one of the first things that we must do to receive salvation.

But what does it say? "The word is near you, in your mouth and in your heart" (that is, the word of faith which we preach):

that if you confess with your mouth the Lord Jesus and believe in your heart that God has raised Him from the dead, you will be saved.

For with the heart one believes unto righteousness, and with the mouth confession is made unto salvation.

For the Scripture says, "Whoever believes on Him will not be put to shame."

Romans 10:8-11

There are several things of the utmost importance in the above verses. Faith involves the confession of the mouth and believing in the heart. The verse clearly states that "if you confess with your lips that Jesus is Lord and believe in your heart that God raised Him from the dead, you will be saved."

Accordingly, I find it very interesting that some Christians actually believe that what comes out of their mouth is irrelevant. Furthermore, another thing I find very interesting is how some Christians will admit this is how one is saved, but then imagine that everything else they receive from God comes differently. The truth is, almost everything one receives from God is received in this manner. Faith is the first thing that leads one to God; it's the last thing a believer will hold onto as they are taken to heaven; and it's extremely important for everything that's done in between.

Faith Comes by Hearing

So faith comes from what is heard, and what is heard comes by the preaching of Christ.

Romans 10:17 (RSV)

I like the Revised Standard Version of this text because it states that faith comes by hearing the preaching of Christ. Christ is the ultimate link between God and man, and as such, He's a teacher, first and foremost. Every recorded word of His inspires faith. Moreover, the entire Bible, as we have it today, is built upon the preaching of Christ (the Anointed One). Thus, one could just as easily say that faith comes by hearing the Word of God.

One might also say that trust and confidence come by hearing the preaching of Christ. Naturally, that makes sense. If we want to get confident about the things of God and confident about what God says, then we need to listen to His words.

Recall from the last chapter that the Word of God is a book of love. As such, it's an unlimited book with unlimited power. We can take the faith filled words of God that are in that Book and reach out into the unlimited realm of the Spirit of God and begin to pull from God's storehouse manifestations of things that He has promised. Faith is essential in this pulling process, because faith takes hold of the promises of God.

Faith refuses to let go. *Faith must be **tenacious**.*

A Visionary Channel

Now faith is the substance of things hoped for, the evidence of things not seen.
Hebrews 11:1

The Amplified Version of this verse says that faith perceives as real what is not revealed to the senses.

As the substance of things hoped for, faith serves as a link between hope and the fulfillment of hope.

Faith can *see* the end result.

Consequently, within faith there is vision.

I like to define faith as a *visionary channel.* In other words, hope is clear images and plans which go past the veil into the throne room of God and give us access, thereby bringing hope into fulfillment. It lays that clear image of hope before the throne room and mercy seat of God, and it proclaims, "God, here is the clear image."

Faith is the *visionary channel* that sees hope grow and reach fulfillment. Hope goes past the veil and into the throne room of God before its plan can be fulfilled. When hope gains access for faith, God sees it and says, "You believed Me. You trusted in Me. You have confidence in Me, and now your hope will be fulfilled."

Many are coming to realize that a church is only as strong as its vision. What some fail to see, however, is that a vision is only as strong as the faith behind it. Moreover, faith is only as strong as our relationship to the author and finisher of faith, the Lord Jesus Christ.

Faith is only as strong as it is close to the Lord Jesus Christ.

There is a genuine intimacy to faith. The more intimate we are with the Word, the more we listen to the Word and obey it. The more we listen to the Word, the more revelation we get of the Word and the more intimacy will be developed.

Breaking the Limits

Faith, by its very nature, goes beyond natural limits. Yet why does our faith seem so limited at times? Almost always it is *we* who set our own limits on our faith, not God. Without a doubt, God is all powerful and all knowing, but He's chosen to reveal Himself according to our faith. In other words, God *is* as our faith will allow Him to be.

If you have trouble believing this, just look at the life of Jesus. Jesus is God incarnate, and all of His actions reflect God. In Matthew 13, you find an excellent example of how He chose to restrict Himself according to the faith of those around Him.

Now He did not do many mighty works there because of their unbelief.

Matthew 13:58

If *we* take the limits off of our faith, we'll take the limits off of our God.

It amazes me how people put limits on so many things. People put a limit on the anointing, as well as God's ability to supply the anointing through us. But if we say, "I can only have faith for so much," we're really saying, "I only trust God this much, I can't trust Him further than that." In this, we put a limit on what God can do and how much we can lean on Him.

Remember, if we're going to have faith in God, we must be willing to break the natural limits.

Great Faith

Now when Jesus had entered Capernaum, a centurion came to Him, pleading with Him,

saying, "Lord, my servant is lying at home paralyzed, dreadfully tormented."

And Jesus said to him, "I will come and heal him."

The centurion answered and said, "Lord, I am not worthy that You should come under my roof. But only speak a word, and my servant will be healed.

"For I also am a man under authority, having soldiers under me. And I say to this one, 'Go,' and he goes; and to another, 'Come,' and he comes; and to my servant, 'Do this,' and he does it."

When Jesus heard it, He marveled, and said to those who followed, "Assuredly, I say to you, I have not found such great faith, not even in Israel!"

Matthew 8:5-10

I believe Jesus characterized the centurion's belief as *great faith* for a couple of reasons. First of all, the man wasn't even an Israelite. As a Gentile, he didn't have the same covenant relationship that the Israelites enjoyed. He was looking into the covenant from the outside. Second, as a soldier and a commander, the man recognized Jesus as one who had authority. Just by being around Him, he knew that Jesus had authority over sickness and disease; and he was quick to trust Jesus' authority!

Third, I believe His faith cut Jesus loose from the limits of time and space, or any other limited formulas. Then, the miracle was accomplished by only a word. The Centurion's faith perceived that Jesus' word had *unlimited* power.

Indeed, that's the essence of great faith. As a result of His faith, Jesus states, "not even in Israel have I found such faith."

The Promise on Board

In Mark four, we find a case in which just the opposite occurs:

> **And a great windstorm arose, and the waves beat into the boat, so that it was already filling.**
>
> **But He was in the stern, asleep on a pillow. And they awoke Him and said to Him, "Teacher, do You not care that we are perishing?"**
>
> **Then He arose and rebuked the wind, and said to the sea, "Peace, be still!" And the wind ceased and there was a great calm.**
>
> **But He said to them, "Why are you so fearful? How is it that you have no faith?"**
>
> **Mark 4:37-40**

Remember that these were Jesus' very own disciples who had witnessed Him perform miracle after miracle. Yet for some reason they still failed to recognize His authority in this matter. Unlike the centurion with great faith, they were not quick to trust in Jesus' authority.

Jesus makes the statement to His disciples, "Why are you afraid? Have you no faith?" When it came to the winds and the waves, the promise was with them in the boat all along.

Did they really think that Jesus would drown in His sleep?

Many people act just like the disciples when the storms of life are raging. They may be in the midst of divorce, or loss of employment, and they cry out, "where is Jesus now, why is He asleep on the bottom of the boat? He doesn't seem to be around while I'm going through my storm." But He is around. He's in the boat where He's supposed to be.

What the disciples failed to realize was that the promise on board *will not drown*.

It might seem like He's asleep on the bottom of the boat, but the promise can't sink. If He's on our boat at all, that means we're not going down. God's promises are yes and amen. How could anyone even think that God's promises would drown when the storm shows up?

As long as God's promise is in the boat, we are not going to drown.

As a Grain of Mustard Seed

Jesus talks about lack of faith, and He talks about little or no faith. Yet I've heard some ministers preach that if you have only a tiny bit of faith, then that's enough. Personally, I'm not comfortable with placing a size on faith, as if it comes in small, medium, or large doses. Faith is faith, regardless of its size. And size is not anymore important than the size of the person that has it. This comes, I believe in part, from a slight mis-translation of Matthew 17:20.

> "…if you have faith as small as a mustard seed, you can say to this mountain, 'move from here to there,' and it will move. Nothing will be impossible for you."
>
> Matthew 17:20 (NIV)

The words *as small as* are not in the Greek manuscript. I believe they were added because the NIV translators misunderstood the concept. Although the NIV is otherwise a fine translation, in this case the New King James, as well as other translations, are closer to the original language. Note this verse according to the New King James:

> "…if you have faith as a mustard seed, you will say to this mountain, 'Move from here to there,' and it will move; and nothing will be impossible for you."
>
> Matthew 17:20

So what's the difference between *as small as* or *as*? I believe the answer lies in another passage from the same book.

> Another parable He put forth to them, saying: "The kingdom of heaven is like a mustard seed, which a man took and sowed in his field,
>
> "which indeed is the least of all the seeds; but when it is grown it is greater than the herbs and becomes a tree, so that the birds of the air come and nest in its branches."
>
> Matthew 13:31,32

What is important about the mustard seed in this passage is the fact that it starts out small but ends up the greatest of shrubs. Thus, it's not the current size that is the emphasis, but the fact that it will *grow*.

This is mustard seed faith, or faith *as* a mustard seed. It starts out small, but within that seed is a blueprint of a giant tree, which also has thousands of more seeds, and in each of those seeds are blueprints of more trees, and the cycle is endless. Therefore this concept, more than anything, explains *unlimited faith*.

Faith as a mustard seed has unlimited potential in it. Just like a mustard seed, there are no boundaries and no limits to it. For example, if you keep adding soil, sunshine, and water to that seed, you can have an *unlimited* amount of mustard trees.

Every seed has this perpetual power. It has the ability to perpetually reproduce.

Jesus correlated faith with a seed. He said if you have faith as, and that means like a seed. What are we going to do if we have faith like a seed? We plant it, we water it, and we give it sunshine so that it will produce. In other words, we *feed* our faith all of the right things.

Jesus was letting us know that our faith has the unlimited potential to multiply and reproduce. Have faith as a seed. Have faith that when you plant, you will expect a harvest. The seed has a perpetual ability to multiply over and over again. If we move a mountain, it will not come back. It is forever moved. If we plant an acorn seed, we are going to have a whole forest available.

Just like the kingdom of heaven, our faith does not stop. God is trying to get us to this unlimited perspective. That means if I speak to sickness by faith and tell it to be moved, the seed will produce, develop, and grow.

When love is our motive, there is no limit to what our faith in God can do.

Placing a Demand

When a seed is placed in the ground, it eventually places a demand on the elements around it. When the tree breaks through and begins to grow, its leaves place a demand on the sun's light. This is called photosynthesis.

Similarly, our faith as it grows must place a demand on the *Son*, Jesus Christ.

How did the woman with the issue of blood get healed? How did her faith heal her?

And suddenly, a woman who had a flow of blood for twelve years came from behind and touched the hem of His garment.

For she said to herself, "If only I may touch His garment, I shall be made well."

But Jesus turned around, and when He saw her He said, "Be of good cheer, daughter; your faith has made you well." And the woman was made well from that hour.

Matthew 9:20-22

She made a confession by faith, and then she reached out and touched God's anointed. With her words *and* her actions she placed a demand on the anointing to flow into her to remove every burden and destroy every yoke, thereby healing her infirmity.

Did her faith act alone? Absolutely not. Her faith was in Jesus. Nevertheless, Jesus did say that her faith made her whole. How did it do this? It functioned as a visionary channel; her faith had a perception.

Faith is the realization of things hoped for and the confidence of things not seen.

By faith, or through the channel of faith, we understand that the worlds were created by a word from God. By faith we know that God sent His Word to heal us. We know that His Word will not return to Him void.

A seed is also like a channel. It is a channel that converts the elements into God's plan for a tree. But that plan will not manifest until the seed places a demand on those elements.

When the proper demand is placed, the seed will continually produce over and over again.

Releasing the Anointing

The anointing will be released according to our faith.

Miracles often depend on whether or not we believe the anointing is there. The woman with the issue of blood believed Jesus was anointed, so she touched His garment. Jesus said, "Your faith has made you whole." Her faith was in what? It was in the fact that Jesus was anointed, and that it could be released through the tip of His garment.

Where did the people of Jesus' time get their faith? They couldn't turn to the Gospels or any of the Epistles. They got it from Jesus' own quotation of an old Testament passage in Isaiah:

"The Spirit of the LORD is upon Me, because He has *anointed* Me to preach the gospel to the poor; He has sent me to heal the broken hearted, to proclaim liberty to the captives and recovery of sight to the blind, to set at liberty those who are oppressed."

Luke 4:18

He said, "I am anointed," and He based it on scripture that most of them knew well. They probably heard Jesus say a number of times, "I am anointed to heal the sick." Then, like the centurion mentioned before, they believed in His authority. Their faith thereby released the anointing they knew He had.

Today, a lot of people attend church meetings, but they don't believe the anointing will flow. They have no faith in either their own or the minister's authority to move in the anointing. As a result, the anointing is not released.

Faith must be in God and His ability to anoint. When a servant of God comes to us, we have to have faith in God's ability to anoint him to remove our burdens and destroy our yokes.

Faith is perception. There's no limit to the perception of faith. It can believe massive things. Note Jesus' own words on this subject:

...anyone who has faith in me will do what I have been doing. He will do even greater things than these, because I am going to the Father.

John 14:12 (NIV)

If Jesus had not said this Himself, it would have been very hard to believe. If we have faith, we'll do what Jesus did; and we'll do greater things than this because He's going to the Father.

Why is that important? We know that since He has gone to the Father, His anointing has come on us.

Faith in His Name

By faith in the name of Jesus, this man whom you see and know was made strong....

Acts 3:16 (NIV)

It's in Jesus' name, and faith in Him, that this man has received his complete healing.

Here we see something different. By now, Jesus has departed and the disciples received the Holy Spirit. We see them operate by faith in His name. They're going forth in His name and with His anointing. There's no limit to what the name of Jesus can do if we have faith that we can go forth in it.

It's not just faith in the anointing, but faith in His name. Through faith in His name, they believed that they were anointed with His anointing. Thus, they were going about healing people in His name.

It was faith in His name that gave this man his healing. But is faith in His name limited to healing?

And whatever you do in word or deed, do all in the name of the Lord Jesus, giving thanks to God the Father through him.

Colossians 3:17

We cannot put a limit on faith in the name of Jesus because according to Second Corinthians 4:13, "we have the same spirit of faith." We have the *same* Unlimited Faith from God that Jesus had. It's a faith that can't be stopped by our enemy. Paul writes in Thessalonians that its growth won't be limited or restricted:

We are bound to thank God always for you, brethren, as it is fitting, because your faith grows exceedingly...

2 Thessalonians 1:3

Smith Wigglesworth was a man who demonstrated unlimited faith in his ministry on earth. He is reported to have raised over twenty people from the dead by the power of God. The following are some of his personal quotes on faith from his book entitled *The Anointing of His Spirit*:

"What is faith? It is the very nature of God. It is the Word of God. It is the personal inward flow of divine favor, which moves in every fiber of our being until our whole nature is so quickened that we live by faith."[2]

"Faith is an increasing position always triumphant, it is not a place of poverty, but of wealth. If you always live in fruitfulness, you will always have plenty."[3]

"If you see imperfect faith, full of doubt, a wavering condition, it always comes because of imperfect knowledge."[4]

"We fail to realize the largeness of our Father's measure and forget that He has a measure, which cannot be exhausted. It pleases Him when we ask for more."[5]

"If you see imperfect faith, you will see imperfect knowledge. Faith comes by hearing and hearing by the Word of God."[6]

Quotes by the Author

"Faith will progress in you from visions, revelations, manifestations; it will continually grow. There's no limit to what faith can do and accomplish when propelled by the unlimited force of love.

"Perfect love can energize unlimited faith. Faith is the audacity that rejoices in the fact that God can't break His own Word.

"If you get strengthened in faith, you won't quit, because faith never gives up.

"Faith is there as long as we're willing to pursue it. There's no limit to the potential of what God can do. We must not put a limit on what God can do inside of us. If we get faith in just one scripture alone, *by His stripes we are healed*, we'll never get sick."

---

[1]Warner, p. 28.

[2]Warner, p. 27.

[3]Warner, p.30.

[4]Warner, p.57.

[5]Warner, p.68.

[6]Warner, p.57.

Chapter 4
Unlimited Anointing

Anointing

The term *anointing* is widely used among Christians today. The very term *Christian* comes from the word Christ. Christ, or *Christos* in Greek, is a term for the Hebrew word *Mashiayach,* or Messiah. *Mashiayach,* or Messiah simply means *anointed one.*[1] Over the last two centuries the word Christ has been misunderstood. Many have come to think of it as a title or name.

To anoint means to pour oil over, or rub oil on something or someone, for the purpose of consecration for service to God. In the Old Testament, anointing with oil was a common practice. Prophets and kings were consecrated for service by having anointing oil poured over their heads by someone acting as God's representative.

During Jesus' lifetime the anticipated coming of Messiah was perhaps the most hotly discussed and debated topic. Many expected the Messiah to be a princely figure who would free Israel from Roman occupation. Christians of course realized that Jesus was God's Anointed One.

The anointing and the Holy Spirit have similar characteristics. Like the Spirit, the anointing has unlimited ability and power because it proceeds from God.

An Unlimited God

In one sense, the anointing could be characterized as God in flesh doing things that only God can do *through* a man. God has chosen to work with and through man (Acts 2:17-18). When the anointing comes into place we're no longer relying on our own power, but rather on God's.

But you have an anointing from the Holy One, and you know all things.

1 John 2:20

The anointing is also considered God's *ability*. The anointing is what flows when one has been anointed, consecrated, and separated unto God.

When Elisha prepared to receive Elijah's anointing, he asked him for the double portion. That's as far as Elisha could see concerning what the anointing could do. He probably would have asked for more, if he had known the anointing could do more.

The anointing will only do what we believe it will do. We need to get a clear understanding of the ability and the power in the anointing because God wants to pour His anointing out in rivers.

The Bible says out of your belly will flow rivers of living water. I believe that's referring to the anointing.

I once heard a minister say that Jesus had so much anointing, but we on the other hand, have only a tiny measure of the anointing.

That's not the case. We're anointed for *His* anointing to flow through us. That means the measure that flows through us is not limited. The channel the anointing flows through might have limitations, but that doesn't mean that the source behind it is also limited.

Think of it like water. Water comes out of a hydrant many times faster than it does out of a faucet. But the supply is still the same. The water that comes out of the hydrant is not better water than that which comes out of the faucet; it is just *more* water.

We limit the unlimited God because we don't see Him as He really is. When we begin to see God as He really is, we'll begin to see the limitlessness of His power that He has imparted to us. Then we'll begin to see the greater demonstrations and manifestations.

1. His Limitless Ability:

Now to Him who is able to do exceedingly abundantly above all that we ask or think, according to the power that works in us,

to Him be glory in the church by Christ Jesus to all generations, forever and ever. Amen.

Ephesians 3:20,21

2. His Limitless Being (nature):

"I am He who lives, and was dead, and behold, I am alive forevermore. Amen. And I have the keys of Hades and of Death."

Revelations 1:18

3. His Limitless Creative Power:

Then God said, "Let there be a firmament in the midst of the waters, and let it divide the waters from the waters."

Thus God made the firmament, and divided the waters which were under the firmament from the waters which were above the firmament; and it was so.

Genesis 1:6,7

All things were made through Him, and without Him nothing was made that was made.

John 1:3

One of the greatest limitations we put on God is not knowing what His will is for us. We have to stop questioning whether or not He and His Word are true or if He will do what He says He will do. In essence, stop being lead by human reasonings that are apart from God, and move into knowing Him. Unlimited anointing will flow out of our intimacy with Him.

In moving in the supernatural, we have to know God's will, not merely wonder whether it's God's will or not. His will is for us to preach the Gospel, heal the sick, cleanse the lepers, raise the dead, and cast out devils.

"And as you go, preach, saying, 'The kingdom of heaven is at hand.'

"Heal the sick, cleanse the lepers, raise the dead, cast out demons. Freely you have received, freely give."

Matthew 10:7,8

We need to give the source free reign to move. We might be bound to a physical body, but the channel for the anointing will grow to the degree that we walk in love and faith. The Bible says, "Christ may dwell in our hearts through faith that we may be rooted and grounded in love." Since Christ means the Anointed, we know that the anointing comes into our hearts through faith and is rooted in love.

How is the anointing going to flow through us? Through faith. Why? Because we are rooted and grounded in love.

God and Flesh

For the earnest expectation of the creation eagerly waits for the revealing of the sons of God.

For the creation was subjected to futility, not willingly, but because of Him who subjected it in hope;

because the creation itself also will be delivered from the bondage of corruption into the glorious liberty of the children of God.

For we know that the whole creation groans and labors with birth pangs together until now.

Not only that, but we also who have the first-fruits of the Spirit, even we ourselves groan within ourselves, eagerly waiting for the adoption, the redemption of our body.

Romans 8:19-23

Creation is groaning, waiting for the manifestation of the sons of God. Notice this is sons with an "s." Jesus was the first begotten of many more to come. When Jesus walked the earth he had power over disease, death, nature, demons, and physical deformities. I believe this was not just authority, but also anointing because in the anointing is power.

Look at the seven sons of Sceva. They thought that by authoritative words they could cast out devils. Scripture reveals that they ran from the demons. Why? Authority without anointing behind it carries no real power. Creation is waiting for us to rise up in the anointing just like Jesus. How can we do greater miracles with less anointing? Is He not the God of increase and multiplication?

The devil attempts to put limits on people's dreams of being used by God through false humility. False humility will try to keep a person down by saying it's wrong to want to be used by God in a great way. The truth is that Jesus said that you would do greater things.

Some say that the flesh is limited; that all depends on the work of sin in the flesh. Remember where Adam failed, Jesus succeeded. We have been redeemed.

Nevertheless death reigned from Adam to Moses, even over those who had not sinned according to the likeness of the transgression of Adam, who is a type of Him who was to come.

But the free gift is not like the offense. For if by the one man's offense many died, much more the grace of God and the gift by the grace of the one Man, Jesus Christ, abounded to many.

And the gift is not like that which came through the one who sinned. For the judgment which came from one offense resulted in condemnation, but the free gift which came from many offenses resulted in justification.

For if by the one man's offense death reigned through the one, much more those who receive abundance of grace and of the gift of righteousness will reign in life through the One, Jesus Christ.

Therefore, as through one man's offense judgment came to all men, resulting in condemnation, even so through one Man's righteous act the free gift came to all men, resulting in justification of life.

> **For as by one man's disobedience many were made sinners, so also by one Man's obedience many will be made righteous.**
>
> **Moreover the law entered that the offense might abound. But where sin abounded, grace abounded much more,**
>
> **so that as sin reigned in death, even so grace might reign through righteousness to eternal life through Jesus Christ our Lord.** Romans 5:14-21

Are we limiting the potential of the restoration of our bodies? Are we saying that the work of the blood within redemption cannot bring us to a place of restoration where the anointing has free room to grow to the point that unlimited anointing can be released?

When Adam sinned he lost his innocence, but when Jesus went to the cross innocence was *restored*.

Innocence can't be found in sin, but innocence can be found in holiness. Innocence has the capacity to contain and release unlimited anointing. "It's God's intention to make us a new creation with all old things passed away and all things within us truly of God, to bring in a new divine order, a perfect love, and an unlimited faith. Will you have it? Redemption is free."[2]

The Bible says, "If you abide in Me and My words abide in you, you shall ask what you desire and it shall be given you."

"Oh Lord," one might say, "I want *unlimited* anointing." When God knows we can handle an unlimited anointing, then He will pour an unlimited anointing through us. He will not shoot something through us that will overload us, nor will he turn up the power level when he knows we can't handle it. If He knows that our love and faith are right and that the channel is set into place and He has free reign to flow through us, then He will do it.

We need to allow the anointed Word to break the stronghold in our minds that used to set limits on God. God's resources are like a spring: they never stop flowing. There's an *unlimited* fountain flowing out of God, and He won't give out of that fountain in measures. Why would He want to give us something limited when He has an unlimited resource?

I'm reminded of an incredible statement from author Myles Munroe in his book *Understanding Your Potential.* "God is always full of power. He has in Him the potential for everything. From the beginning, God gave that same ability to be potent to all His creation. He planted within each person or thing He created, including you, the ability to be much more than it is at any one moment. Thus God created you to be omnipotent."[3]

I once heard Gloria Copeland say that "the anointing is the kingdom of God bursting in upon this natural realm and bringing God's free favors profusely." Profusely means lavishly, liberally, extravagantly, and over and abounding. This mentality should be evident in our ministry. We have to minister so that people have the ability and freedom to do what God has told them to do. We can't put a cap on someone's potential. He wants us to have His resurrection life, His energy force. He wants us to be recipients of His life so that His Spirit will flow through us. We need to come to and remain in the place where we don't limit these things.

The anointing in us works a little like light on a ruby. The ruby is tinted red with thousands of refracted indexes. When that light beam hits a ruby, it begins to bounce within the ruby. By the time the light comes out of the other side, it comes out as a laser beam. The laser beam can be so powerful that it can shoot a plane out of the sky or do surgery. But the power that is coming out of the other side of the ruby is greater than the power that went into the ruby.

Jesus said, "The works that I do shall you do also and greater works shall you do, because I go unto the Father."

Greater is He that is in us, than He that is in the world. We have a treasure in earthen vessels that the excellency of power may be of God and not of man.

For additional information on this matter, please read my book, *Transparency*.

Our Destiny

Destiny is living inside of us. God has anointed, separated, and consecrated us. Now you might not accept that anointing, that consecration and separation, but God has destined us to be separated (set apart). He has destined us to be a living vessel and channel full of His potential, growing in faith and believing on the Lord Jesus Christ in faith. We will then come into the Lord Jesus Christ so that the anointing and power and glory can flow out of us.

There's no limit to the levels of glory that can flow out of us because we are looking at the mirror of Christ, the Anointed One, who is in us. In the anointing dwells the fullness of unlimited power. Within the anointing is the seed of unlimited perpetual power. We are the seed of Christ. Every time we look at ourselves, God wants us to see ourselves in a *greater* dimension of son-ship and authority that He has called us to.

Now the Lord is the Spirit; and where the Spirit of the Lord is, there is liberty.

> **But we all, with unveiled face, beholding as in a mirror the glory of the Lord, are being transformed into the same image from glory to glory, just as by the Spirit of the Lord.**
>
> **2 Corinthians 3:17,18**

We're called to be a royal priesthood and peculiar generation, set apart by God, a King's kid and one who is in covenant relationship with almighty God. He has called us to a higher place than we could ever imagine or dream.

The Bible says in Job 29:6 that Job's steps were bathed with cream, and the rock poured out rivers of oil for him. This was the Old Testament, and we're under a better covenant. How much more should the anointing be available to us?

God doesn't put a limit on His anointing. He doesn't try to stop what He Himself has planned from the foundation of the world. All things are possible to him who believes. How can we say that there's a limited anointing? How can we do greater miracles and greater works than Jesus did with less anointing? We can't.

According to Joel 2, He is going to pour out His Spirit upon all flesh. Your sons and daughters shall prophesy, your old men will dream dreams, your young men shall see visions. God will give us visions and dreams because that's where God shows us impossible things. He wouldn't allow us the ability to have an unction from the Holy One, who knows all things, if He doesn't want to show an anointing that has unlimited dimensions.

Why would He put limits on His anointing if He knows all things? *All* means it encompasses everything and that which is beyond limits. God is a God of increase and multiplication.

Behold, how good and how pleasant it is for brethren to dwell together in unity!

It is like the precious oil upon the head, running down on the beard, the beard of Aaron, running down on the edge of his garments.

It is like the dew of Hermon, descending upon the mountains of Zion; for there the LORD commanded the blessing — life forevermore.

Psalms 133:1-3

The precious oil is flowing from Jesus. He is the head. It flows from the head to the garments; the oil is no less. The same oil that flows on the head is flowing on the garments of the body. It did not say it was a weaker anointing, or a lesser anointing.

"And the glory which You gave Me I have given them, that they may be one just as We are one."

John 17:22

According to this verse, did He give us less glory? No. It says that He gave us the *same* glory. I once heard Myles Munroe say, "Whatever you come out of, is an indication of your potential"(unlimited power).

I can do all things through the potential of the Anointed One's anointing that's infusing me.

"For He whom God has sent speaks the words of God, for God does not give the Spirit by measure."

John 3:34

..."Peace to you! As the Father has sent Me, I also send you."

John 20:21

Or as another translation says: The same way I was sent, you will be sent also.

59

How is that? Is He going to send us with less than what He was sent with? How did the Father send Jesus? Equipped. How will He send us? He sends us the same way. If we are called to do the same works and greater, then we will need the same equipping. Christ in us is the hope of glory.

There is an Anointed One in us who is the earnest expectation of the manifestation of the Word. What is glory? Glory is the Word becoming flesh. The anointing is responsible for the Word becoming flesh, and we must step beyond the activating or the awakening of truth and into the Word becoming flesh.

We need to step into a greater, unlimited dimension, a greater ability and power. We need to go further with God than we've ever gone before.

Laying Hold of Our Inheritance

God is all-powerful. Jesus wants to bring us to an age of maturity, a place of accountability where we *know* that we're seated with Christ in heavenly places. We are joint heirs with Christ. We've been sealed with the Holy Spirit of promise. We've been made partakers of His divine inheritance.

Do you think that He has a limit to His divine inheritance?

He says in Second Peter 1:4 that we have been made partakers of His divine nature. How can we get a hold of God's nature and say that part of God's nature is limited.

"I just got a *part* of God's nature." Even if that were the case, is it a limited part? Even if we had one/one billionth of God's nature, there's still unlimited power in that tiny fraction of God's nature.

There's no part of God's nature that has only limited potential in it. Every particle of God has unlimited power and potential and unlimited anointing in it. If we just have one little dot of God, we have unlimited power and anointing, because God is God.

We need to stop binding God to something that's limited. That's what man-made religion sometimes does. It can't grow arms and legs or raise the dead. It can't do anything.

What we need is a creative power, a creative God living inside of us doing omnipotent, omniscient, and all-powerful things.

I press on that I may lay hold of that which Christ Jesus has laid hold of for me. Why would Paul say that if He did not want to get it?

Because of Colossians 2:8, some people don't know what their divine inheritance is. They're not going to lay hold of anything or get what God has for them if they don't go for it.

Brethren, I do not count myself to have appre-hended; but one thing I do, forgetting those things which are behind and reaching forward to those things which are ahead,

I press toward the goal for the prize of the upward call of God in Christ Jesus.

Philippians 3:13,14

A Perfect Man

I want all that God has for me. I want all that God can give me. I want all the fullness of God. I *do not* want to set a limit on God. I want God to move, flow, and have His way. I want Christ's, the Anointed One's, anointing to have full reign and rule in my life.

for the equipping of the saints for the work of ministry, for the edifying of the body of Christ,

till we all come to the unity of the faith and of the knowledge of the Son of God, to a perfect man, to the measure of the stature of the fullness of Christ.

Ephesians 4:12-13

What is a perfect man? It's a man to the measure of the stature of the fullness of Christ. That's the only place measure means a measure.

What is the measure here? The fullness of the stature of Christ.

Yea doubtless, and I count all things but loss for the excellency of the knowledge of Christ Jesus my Lord: for whom I have suffered the loss of all things, and do count them but dung, that I may win Christ,

And be found in him, not having mine own righteousness, which is of the law, but that which is through the faith of Christ, the righteousness which is of God by faith:

That I may know him, and the power of his resurrection, and the fellowship of his sufferings, being made conformable unto his death;

If by any means I might attain unto the resurrection of the dead.

Not as though I had already attained, either were already perfect: but I follow after, if that I may apprehend that for which also I am apprehended of Christ Jesus.

Philippians 3:8-12 (KJV)

Basically Paul is saying I count all things as loss to the excellency of Christ that I may come to the fullness of Christ.

The limit here is the *fullness*. If we have the fullness we will raise the dead and heal the sick. Until we do that, we'd better keep growing. As far as the world is concerned, we're dead, and our lives are hidden with Christ in God.

When Jesus called His disciples together in Matthew 10:1, He gave them power over unclean spirits to cast them out and to heal all kinds of sickness and all kinds of disease. He didn't give them power to heal only a *few* sicknesses and *some* diseases. He gave them power to heal *all* sickness and *all* disease. God has given us *authority* over all sickness and all disease.

Ask Anything

We need to expect one hundred percent results. We need to expect one hundred percent miracles and healings and one hundred percent release of the anointing.

We don't need to settle for anything less than the unlimited realms of God's glory.

"For assuredly, I say to you, whoever says to this mountain, 'Be removed and be cast into the sea,' and does not doubt in his heart, but believes that those things he says will be done, he will have whatever he says.

"Therefore I say to you, whatever things you ask when you pray, believe that you receive them, and you will have them."
Mark 11:23,24

"Ask, and it will be given to you; seek, and you will find; knock, and it will be opened to you.

"For everyone who asks receives, and he who seeks finds, and to him who knocks it will be opened."
Matthew 7:7,8

"Again I say to you that if two of you agree on earth concerning anything that they ask, it will be done for them by My Father in heaven."

Matthew 18:19

"You did not choose Me, but I chose you and appointed you that you should go and bear fruit, and that your fruit should remain, that whatever you ask the Father in My name He may give you."

John 15:16

If any of you lacks wisdom, let him ask of God, who gives to all liberally and without reproach, and it will be given to him.

James 1:5

You lust and do not have. You murder and covet and cannot obtain. You fight and war. Yet you do not have because you do not ask.

You ask and do not receive, because you ask amiss, that you may spend it on your pleasures.

James 4:2,3

And whatever we ask we receive from Him, because we keep His commandments and do those things that are pleasing in His sight.

1 John 3:22

And we have seen and testify that the Father has sent the Son as Savior of the world.

Whoever confesses that Jesus is the Son of God, God abides in him, and he in God.

1 John 4:14,15

We don't need to settle for anything less than submitting to the full potential of the anointing to flow in and out of us.

If the anointing moving through us is not healing all kinds of disease and all kinds of sickness just as Jesus did, then we need to start keeping our eyes fixed on Him and our minds focused on Him, because we're still growing.

God desires to move through us in an unlimited dimension. Take note of what Jesus says to His disciples not long before His crucifixion:

"...The words that I speak to you I do not speak on My own authority; but the Father who dwells in Me does the works.

"Believe Me that I am in the Father and the Father in Me, or else believe Me for the sake of the works themselves.

"Most assuredly, I say to you, he who believes in Me, the works that I do he will do also; and greater works than these he will do, because I go to My Father.

"And whatever you ask in My name, that I will do, that the Father may be glorified in the Son.

"If you ask anything in My name, I will do it."

John 14:10-14

Do you believe that you can receive an unlimited anointing? This is unlimited thinking. The same anointing that flows through Jesus flows through us. It's an unlimited supply. There's nothing that can stop it except the limits that you put into place.

"If you love Me, keep My commandments.

"And I will pray the Father, and He will give you another Helper, that He may abide with you forever —

"the Spirit of truth, whom the world cannot receive, because it neither sees Him nor knows Him; but you know Him, for He dwells with you and will be in you.

"I will not leave you orphans; I will come to you.

"A little while longer and the world will see Me no more, but you will see Me. Because I live, you will live also.

"At that day you will know that I am in My Father, and you in Me, and I in you."

John 14:15-20

There's no limit to that.

God doesn't have just a tiny part for you. In the natural, do our children have any less ability than we do? No, they have the potential to become all that we are. So, as the children of God, we have the potential to become all that He is, through Jesus Christ our Lord.

Anointed to Take Nations

I have raised him up in righteousness, and I will direct all his ways; he shall build My city and let My exiles go free, not for price nor reward," says the LORD of hosts.

Thus says the LORD: "The labor of Egypt and merchandise of Cush and of the Sabeans, men of stature, shall come over to you, and they shall be yours; they shall walk behind you, they shall come over in chains; and they shall bow down to you. They will make supplication to you, saying,

'Surely God is in you, and there is no other; there is no other God.'"

Isaiah 45:13,14

"Thus says the LORD to His anointed, to Cyrus, whose right hand I have held — to subdue nations before him and loose the armor of kings, to open before him the double doors, so that the gates will not be shut:

'I will go before you and make the crooked places straight; I will break in pieces the gates of bronze and cut the bars of iron.

'I will give you the treasures of darkness and hidden riches of secret places, that you may know that I, the LORD, who call you by your name, am the God of Israel.

'For Jacob My servant's sake, and Israel My elect, I have even called you by your name; I have named you, though you have not known Me.

'I am the LORD, and there is no other; there is no God besides Me. I will gird you, though you have not known Me.'"

Isaiah 45:1-5

It is God's anointing that is subduing the nations.

Cyrus could subdue nations because he was *anointed*. God gave him the strength.

He began with Persia and (according to the Jamieson, Fausset, and Brown Commentary) he expanded to Media, Bactria, Lydia, Elam, with Susiana, Asia Minor, Babylonia and Assyria, Samaria, and Judea. From several successful expeditions in Central Asia, it's probable that he contemplated the extension of his conquests to the Indus River. These, without mentioning many smaller dependencies, constituted the widespread Persian Empire of which Cyrus was the mighty ruler.

When God says that he held Cyrus' right hand it means that He strengthened him.

Likewise, when He holds our hands He strengthens us. God will enable us to take the nations with His unlimited anointing.

Verse four of the same chapter tells us that God did this for the sake of Israel.

Now in the first year of Cyrus king of Persia, that the word of the LORD by the mouth of Jeremiah might be fulfilled, the LORD stirred up the spirit of Cyrus king of Persia, so that he made a proclamation throughout all his kingdom, and also put it in writing, saying,

Thus says Cyrus king of Persia: All the kingdoms of the earth the LORD God of heaven has given me. And He has commanded me to build Him a house at Jerusalem which is in Judah.

Who is among you of all His people? May his God be with him, and let him go up to Jerusalem which is in Judah, and build the house of the LORD God of Israel (He is God), which is in Jerusalem.

And whoever is left in any place where he dwells, let the men of his place help him with silver and gold, with goods and livestock, besides the freewill offerings for the house of God which is in Jerusalem.

Ezra 1:1-4

The Israelite leaders had been in Babylonian captivity for many years before the Persian King Cyrus conquered Babylon. According to Ezra 5:13, it was during

Cyrus' first year of his acquisition of Babylon that he allowed them to return to rebuild the temple.

Working Together

In conclusion: It's interesting how all these chapters are interrelated. Yet that's often the case with the things of God, they're often interrelated and dependent upon each other. For instance, faith is essential, but it must work through love. When the love of God is shed abroad in our hearts a new nature begins to develop within us, the nature of a forgiver.

As we move in unlimited forgiveness it releases the power and anointing of God to flow. However, unbelief, hatred, and unforgiveness all hinder and stop the flow of God's power. Why? Because God's power reaches us through Christ's anointing, and Christ was the ultimate believer, lover, and forgiver. Hatred, unbelief, and unforgiveness are completely opposed to Him. In Christ dwells the fullness of the Godhead bodily. That means *Jehovah Raphah*, the Lord my healer. In *Jehovah Raphah,* I receive unlimited healing.

In the anointing, there's unlimited provision; *Jehovah Jireh*, the Lord my provider.

In the anointing, there's unlimited victory; *Jehovah Nissi*, the Lord my Victory.

In the anointing, there's unlimited peace, *Jehovah Shalom*.

In the anointing, there's unlimited presence, *Jehovah Shammah*. God said that He would never leave us nor forsake us.

In the anointing, there's unlimited sanctification, *Jehovah Makkadesh*, the Lord my sanctifier.

In the anointing, dwells the fullness of the Godhead bodily, it's unlimited provision for everything we're ever in need of.

In unlimited knowledge and unlimited vision what is clearly heard and seen will cause faith to grow beyond limits.

We know that power without compassion can accomplish nothing, but power with unlimited love can accomplish the impossible. It's love that gives faith the ability to move mountains.

When you yield to unlimited forgiveness working in your life, you allow unlimited love to energize unlimited faith, thus allowing unlimited anointing to remove every burden and destroy every yoke making way for the fruit of glory to be produced.

---

[1]Walter Bauer, *A Greek English Lexicon of the New Testament* (Chicago: The University of Chicago Press, 1979), pp. 311, 859.

[2]Warner, p.57.

[3]Myles Munroe, *Understanding Your Potential* (Destiny Image, 1991), p. 23.

The Vision of Sword Ministries

The foundation of this ministry rests in Hebrews 4:12 which is summarized in the following statement, "Speaking the Truth in Revival, Piercing the Innermost Being." We are to remain carriers of revival, "Demonstrating Signs and Wonders, Decently and In Order, by the Power of the Holy Spirit."

Our vision is to see the stadiums of America and around the world filled to capacity in which the fullness of the Gospel of Christ, the Anointed One is declared unto salvation. Not just in persuasive words of man's wisdom, but in demonstration of the Spirit and in Power (Acts 2), which includes salvation according to Acts 10:44.

To see multitudes touched by the loving presentation of the power of God through power packed spirit filled books published in many different languages, world wide multi-media television and radio productions, and churches and Bible schools established in China and other nations, via Apostolic teams and multi-faceted Evangelistic operations.